THE FACTS ON
JESUS
THE
M...

John Ankerberg
& John Weldon

HARVEST HOUSE PUBLISHERS
Eugene, Oregon 97402

Other books by John Ankerberg and John Weldon

The Facts on Astrology
The Facts on Creation vs. Evolution
The Facts on the Faith Movement
The Facts on False Teaching in the Church
The Facts on Hinduism
*The Facts on Holistic Health
and the New Medicine*
The Facts on Islam
The Facts on the Jehovah's Witnesses
The Facts on Jesus the Messiah
The Facts on Life After Death
The Facts on the Masonic Lodge
The Facts on the Mind Sciences
The Facts on the Mormon Church
The Facts on the New Age Movement
The Facts on the Occult
The Facts on Rock Music
The Facts on Roman Catholicism
The Facts on Sex Education
The Facts on Spirit Guides
*The Facts on UFO's and
Other Supernatural Phenomena*

THE FACTS ON JESUS THE MESSIAH

Copyright © 1993 by The Ankerberg
   Theological Research Institute
Published by Harvest House Publishers
Eugene, Oregon 97402

ISBN 1-56507-109-3

This material constitutes a condensed and revised version of portions of the authors' book, *The Case for Jesus the Messiah* (Eugene, OR: Harvest House, 1989; updated and expanded, Baker Book House, 1993) which supplies additional important details and responds to specific questions of critics.

Printed in the United States of America.

Contents

Preface
Solving a Mystery

Preface

[Jesus] said to them, "How foolish you are, and how slow of heart to believe all that the prophets have spoken! Did not the Christ [Messiah] have to suffer these things and then enter His glory?" And beginning with Moses and all the Prophets, he explained to them what was said in all the Scriptures concerning himself (Luke 24:25-27, NIV).

The things which God announced beforehand by the mouth of all the prophets, that His Christ [Messiah] should suffer, He has thus fulfilled (Acts 3:18, NASB).

[If we examine] those passages in the Old Testament to which the ancient synagogue referred to as Messianic... [we find] upwards of 456... and their Messianic application is supported by more than 558 references to the most ancient rabbinic writings.... A careful perusal of their Scripture quotations show that the main postulates of the New Testament concerning the Messiah are fully supported by rabbinic statements (Alfred Edersheim, a teacher of languages and Warbutonian Lecturer at Lincoln's Inn [Oxford], Grinfield Lecturer on the Septuagint, *The Life and Times of Jesus the Messiah*, Vol. 1, 163-164).

Jesus of Nazareth changed the world. Never has there been a man like Him, and never will there be. He is the subject of more books, plays, poetry, films, and worship than any man in human history. To read His words carefully—alongside those of Muhummad, Buddha, the Hindu scriptures, or those of any other religious leader—is to be confounded by their power and uniqueness. Those who heard Him asked in astonishment, "Where did this man get this wisdom and these miraculous powers?" (Matthew 13:54, NIV). And to look at what He *did* is to be convinced intuitively of the basic claims of Christian faith. As the famous writer Malcolm Muggeridge observed, "The words of the Gospels... in the truest and most absolute sense... may be called Holy Words, and without blasphemy, attributed to God Himself."[1]

Whatever good Christianity has done for the world has come because of Jesus. But who was this man? The purpose of this book is to show how the Hebrew Scriptures predicted

4

centuries in advance the coming of a divine Messiah for all mankind, and that Jesus is the fulfillment of those prophecies.

Some have claimed that these statements were made after Jesus lived, not before. But the entire Hebrew Scriptures were completed by 400 B.C. And no matter what your view of the Hebrew Scriptures, one fact is unassailable: The Septuagint, the Greek translation of the entire Hebrew Scriptures, was completed by 247 B.C.

Therefore, even critics must acknowledge that every prophecy we will discuss in this book, and many more, were in existence well in advance of the time Jesus lived—in fact, at least some 250 years before He was even born.

We will also show that the Messiah is spoken of in such specific detail in the Hebrew Scriptures that it is literally impossible to account for such predictions apart from the Bible being a divine revelation of God to humanity.

There are those today who reject this conclusion, but they refuse to consider the prophecies fairly and on their own merit. Only a preexisting bias against supernatural prophecy itself (such as those holding a rationalistic worldview) or a bias against these prophecies referring to the person of Jesus can deter someone from accepting the Scriptures as Messianic.

We have written this book to set forth a small portion of the evidence found in the Hebrew Scriptures that predicted the coming of the Messiah. We believe God gave this evidence so that those who are willing to allow the facts to speak for themselves will be able to discover the truth.

Solving a Mystery

Is there evidence in history that God gave specific information hundreds of years in advance about a person He knew would live? What specific accounts are given and where can they be found? Did the people to whom the information came recognize that they had been given special information? Do these prophecies constitute solid evidence for us today? Is it possible for us to account for this information apart from the fact it must have come from God? And did the Jewish community before and after Christ believe these same Hebrew Scriptures pointed to a coming Messiah?

The prophecies in the Old Testament are like clues in a mystery story. In this book we will try to gather enough clues to identify the special person who is talked about in the Hebrew Scriptures. As we shall see, the clues will lead us to ask:

- Who is the seed (offspring) of the woman who crushes the head of Satan?
- Who is the seed of Abraham, Isaac, and Jacob that will eventually bless all nations?
- Who is the "prophet like Moses" of whom God says, "You must listen to him"?
- Who is the one crucified?
- Who is the *child* that is God and will have an everlasting kingdom?
- Who was crushed and pierced for our transgressions? Upon whom did the Lord lay the iniquity of all mankind?
- Who is the righteous Branch, the wise King, who will be called "the Lord our righteousness"?
- Who is the "Anointed One" to be "cut off" after 483 years?
- Who is the one who is eternal, who will be the ruler over Israel, who is born in Bethlehem Ephrathah?
- Who is Jehovah, "the one they have pierced," for whom Jerusalem and all the nation of Israel will weep and mourn?

No one can deny that the Bible itself claims to be the unique revelation of God: "All Scripture is inspired by God and profitable for teaching, for reproof, for correction, for training in righteousness; that the man of God may be adequate, equipped for every good work" (2 Timothy 3:16,17, NASB). If you do not agree, the material discussed in this book should be of interest to you, because the Bible's claim to uniqueness and the prophecies of a future Messiah go together. If the prophecies are truly fulfilled, then the Bible has provided information about the future that could only have come from God.

We are aware that some people have applied different interpretations to these prophetic verses, but we are convinced that such interpretations result from misinterpretation or biased assumptions that will not allow the evidence to speak for itself.[2,14]

Before we examine the prophecies themselves, however, we want to document the fact that God did promise to give information through His prophets concerning the future.

1. Did God promise to speak through His prophets things concerning the future?

God did promise to speak through His prophets. In fact, He said this would be proof that He was God, indeed, the true God for all the earth. He even challenged one and all to make statements about the future that would be as accurate as His statements about the future:

> Who then is like me? Let him proclaim it. Let him declare and lay out before me what has happened ...and what is yet to come—yes, let him foretell what will come....*Did I not proclaim this and foretell it long ago?* (Isaiah 44:7,8, NIV, emphasis added).

> Who *foretold this long ago*, who declared it from the distant past? Was it not I, the LORD? (Isaiah 45:21, NIV, emphasis added).

It is significant that in the most Messianic of all the Hebrew Scriptures, Isaiah, God speaks most frequently of His ability to predict the future. He challenges the false gods (idols) and their prophets to prove their case.

For example:

> Declare to us *the things to come*, tell us what the future holds, so that we may know that you are gods (Isaiah 41:22,23, NIV, emphasis added).

> *I foretold* the former things long ago, my mouth announced them and I made them known; then suddenly I acted, and they came to pass....Therefore I

told you these things long ago; *before they happened* I announced them to you *so that* you could not say, "My idols did them" (Isaiah 48:3,5, NIV, emphasis added).

The New Testament also claims that the ancient Hebrew prophets spoke by the inspiration of God: "Above all, you must understand that no prophecy of Scripture came about by the prophet's own interpretation. For prophecy never had its origin in the will of man, *but men spoke from God* as they were carried along by the Holy Spirit" (2 Peter 1:20,21, NIV, emphasis added).

It makes the further claim that the ancient prophets, whose writings spanned a thousand years, were all in agreement concerning a specific future Person: "*All the prophets testify* about *him* that everyone who believes in him receives forgiveness of sins through his name" (Acts 10:43, NIV, emphasis added). And, "So I stand here and testify to small and great alike. I am saying nothing beyond what *the prophets and Moses said* would happen—that the Christ [Messiah] would suffer and, as the first to rise from the dead, would proclaim light to his own people and to the Gentiles" (Acts 26:22,23, NIV, emphasis added).

2. What is the definition of the word Messiah?

The word *Messiah* is taken from Psalm 2:2 and Daniel 9:25,26 where *Mashiyach* (Hebrew), *Christos* (Greek) means "Anointed One." The term takes its meaning from the Jewish practice of "anointing" prophets, priests, and kings to their respective offices. For example, as a generic term it could be applied to an earthly king such as David (2 Samuel 19:21) who was "anointed" to fulfill the divine purpose of his office.

However, there was one unique individual to whom the term *Messiah* applied in a special sense. God spoke about a future ruler of Israel who would sit on the throne of David and usher in an age of unparalleled righteousness and peace. He would simultaneously hold all three offices of prophet (authoritative proclamation), priest (spiritual duties), and king (political ruler). He would be the reality and ultimate fulfillment to which all other usages of the term *Messiah* would be but shadowy prefigures.[3]

This would be the one to come whom God would uniquely identify beforehand. As the apostle Peter wrote, "But this is how God fulfilled *what he had foretold* through all the prophets, saying that his Christ [Messiah] would suffer" (Acts 3:18, NIV, emphasis added).

3. If specific prophecies were fulfilled by the Messiah, does the science of probability consider this "proof" there is a God?

Anyone can *make* predictions—that is easy. Having them fulfilled is another story. The more statements you make about the future and the greater the detail, the better the chances are that you will be proven wrong.

For example, how difficult do you think it would be to indicate the precise kind of death that a new, unknown religious leader would experience a thousand years from today? Could you describe and predict a new method of execution not currently known—one that won't even be invented for hundreds of years? That's what David did in 1000 B.C. when he wrote Psalm 22.

Further, if you did think up 50 specific prophecies about some man in the future you will never meet, how difficult do you think it would be for that man to fulfill all 50 of your predictions? How hard would it be for him if 25 of your predictions were about what *other* people would do to him and were completely beyond his control?

It might be possible to arrange one or two of these prophecies, but it would be virtually impossible for any man to arrange and fulfill all these predictions in advance. If it can be proved that such prophecies were predicted of the Messiah hundreds of years in advance, and one man fulfilled *all* of them, then that man would logically have to be the Messiah.

God gave a great number of prophecies (more than 400) about the Messiah for at least two reasons. First, it would make identifying the Messiah obvious. And second, it would make an imposter's task impossible.

Now let us ask an intriguing question. If we assume some 456 prophecies are fulfilled in one person, what does the science of probability say about this? In brief, it says, if accurate predictions were made about a future Messiah and fulfilled years later by one person, this is reasonable proof that there is a God.

Here is why. The science of probability attempts to determine the chance that a given event will occur. Professor Emeritus of Science at Westmont College, Peter Stoner, has calculated the probability of one man fulfilling some of the major prophecies made concerning the Messiah. The estimates were worked out by 12 different classes of 600 college students.

The students carefully weighed all the factors, discussed each prophecy at length, and examined the various circumstances which might indicate that men had conspired together to fulfill a particular prophecy. They made their estimates conservative enough so that there was, finally, unanimous agreement even among the skeptical students.

But then Professor Stoner took their estimates and made them even more conservative. He also encouraged other skeptics or scientists to make their own estimates to see if his conclusions were more than fair. Finally, he submitted his figures for review to a Committee of the American Scientific Affiliation. Upon examination, they verified that his calculations were dependable and accurate in regard to the scientific material presented.[4]

After examining *eight* different prophecies, Professor Stoner and his students conservatively estimated that the chance of one man fulfilling all eight prophecies was one in 10^{17}.

To show how large the number 10^{17} is (a figure with 17 zeros), Stoner gave this illustration. Imagine covering the entire state of Texas with silver dollars to a level of two feet deep. The total number of silver dollars needed to cover the whole state would be 10^{17}. Now, choose just one of those silver dollars, mark it, and drop it from an airplane. Then thoroughly stir all the silver dollars all over the state.

When that has been done, blindfold one man, then tell him he can travel wherever he wishes in the state of Texas. But sometime he must stop, reach down into the two feet of silver dollars, and try to pull up that one specific silver dollar that has been marked.

Now, the chance of his finding that one silver dollar in the state of Texas would be the chance the prophets had for eight of their prophecies coming true in any one man in the future.

Professor Stoner concluded: "The fulfillment of these eight prophecies alone proves that God inspired the writing of those prophecies to a definiteness which lacks only one chance in 10^{17} of being absolute."[5] Another way of saying this is that any person who minimizes or ignores the significance of the biblical identifying signs concerning the Messiah would be foolish.

But, of course, there are many more than eight prophecies. In another calculation Stoner used 48 prophecies (even though he could have used 456) and arrived at the extremely conservative estimate that the probability of 48 prophecies being fulfilled in one person is 10^{157}.

And how big is 10^{157}? In 10^{157} years, an ant could actually move *all* the atoms in 600,000 trillion, trillion, trillion, trillion of our universes a distance of 200,000,000,000, 000,000,000 miles. He could do this moving *one* atom at a time, moving each atom a distance of 30 billion light years, and traveling only at the speed of one inch every 15 billion years![6]

This incredibly large number illustrates why it is impossible for anyone to have fulfilled *all* the Messianic prophecies by chance. In fact, a leading authority on probability theory, Emile Borel, states in his book *Probabilities and Life*, that once we go past one chance in 10^{50}, the probabilities are so small it's impossible to think they will ever occur.[7] (10^{157} is almost infinitely beyond 10^{50}.)

What all this means is it is impossible for these 48 prophecies to be fulfilled apart from divine prediction. This is proof that there must be a God who supernaturally gave this information. The question is, can it be shown that such prophecies do, in fact, exist?

We will now examine several prophetic passages that give us specific statements about the Messiah. As you read through them, ask yourself the following questions: Is this truly a prophecy about a future person? Does Jesus Christ fulfill it and no one else? How was it possible for each of these prophecies to find fulfillment in one man hundreds of years in the future? In other words, if each prophecy is admitted to be about the Messiah and Jesus Christ fulfills all the prophecies, isn't this proof that Jesus is the Messiah?

4. Genesis 3:15—Who is the seed (offspring) of the woman who crushes the head of Satan?

The Biblical Text (1400 B.C.)

> So the Lord God said to the serpent, "Because you have done this...I will put enmity between you and the woman, and between your seed and her seed. He will bruise your head, and you will bruise his heel" (Genesis 3:14,15).

The Context of This Passage

The context of this passage is the temptation and Fall of Adam and Eve by the deception of "the serpent." Who is "the serpent"? Revelation 12:9 and 20:2 identifies him as "the serpent of old," "the devil," or "Satan."

For those who accept only the Hebrew Scriptures as authoritative, the serpent in Genesis 3:14 cannot be just an animal. The *serpent* must be a *person*. The word *enmity* in the Hebrew Scriptures is a specialized word that *always* refs to hatred between persons.[8] It is never used to describe enmity between an animal and a person.

In this passage Satan has already deceived Adam and Eve. All three are now being addressed by God. What God says is astonishing!

The Explanation of the Text

Carefully examining this text, we find a number of things: God is speaking to the serpent, who is not an animal and is identified in the book of Revelation as "Satan." God says He will put enmity (irreconcilable hatred) between the serpent (Satan) and the woman. God says this enmity will spread to the serpent's seed and the woman's seed. But then God suddenly speaks specifically of "one" of Eve's seed, a "he,"* a male descendant. God announces this one, "he," will someday bruise the head of the serpent (Satan), and Satan will bruise his heel.

So there are five participants spoken of in this verse: 1) Satan; 2) the woman; 3) Satan's seed; 4) the woman's seed; and 5) finally, one *from* the woman's seed, the "he" who bruises Satan's head but is bruised in the heel by Satan.

What does it mean for the male descendant of the woman to "bruise" Satan's head? Translators have rendered the Hebrew word *bruise* as "crush."[9] This is because it more clearly fits both the meaning of the word and the context. The actual Hebrew word means to "break or smite in pieces; greatly to injure or wound."[10]

Though the same Hebrew word is used (both the head and heel are "crushed"), we see that one of the wounds is irreversibly fatal, the other is not. Why? The reason is the location of the crushing. In the head, this is irreparable—it is too vital an organ to survive being crushed. But this is not true for the heel. To crush someone's heel is to inflict a serious but not irreparable wound.

If a man steps on a snake's *head*, it will be irreversibly crushed—thus the imagery points to the serpent's wound as being fatal. On the other hand, a crushed *heel* may be nursed back to health. This is why the great Hebrew scholar Franz Delitzsch has said this verse is teaching "the definite promise of victory over the serpent...because it suffers the deadly tread."[11] In brief, God is saying the male seed of the woman will be victorious over Satan because he (the serpent) will be mortally wounded.

---

* The King James version made a mistake here. The translators ignored the third person masculine, singular pronoun, and so wrote "it." But the grammar clearly indicates "he."

Does Eve's male descendant in this verse refer to the person of Jesus Christ? It is clear that it must refer to some future man and, as we will see, God Himself will add other identifying signs to answer this question. Jesus does fit the requirements spoken of here. Jesus Himself said that He had come to destroy the works of the devil (John 12:31; 16:11; cf. Hebrews 2:14; 1 John 3:8). Has anyone else in human history ever made such a claim? When Jesus died on the cross, He provided and made available salvation for all mankind (John 3:16). He broke the power Satan had exercised over all humanity, and now provides victory over sin and the devil. Because of Jesus' death on the cross and His resurrection, He inflicted a fatal blow to the devil's domination over man (Acts 10:38; 26:15-18; Ephesians 4:8; Colossians 2:15; James 4:7). In the future, at Jesus' second coming, He will permanently defeat the devil by removing him from the earth and casting him into hell forever (Romans 16:20; Revelation 20:10). The text also talks of the seed (offspring) of the serpent and the seed (offspring) of the woman.

The offspring of Satan would refer to the demons or fallen angels who followed Satan in his rebellion. All through Scripture we are told that "Satan's seed" tries to destroy humanity (John 8:44; Revelation 12:9; 16:14). The "seed of the woman" obviously would refer to all her children, to all humanity.*

God describes the scope of the conflict. It will involve all future generations, "between your [Satan's] seed and her [the woman's] seed" (1 Peter 5:8; 1 John 5:19).

Satan's success in deceiving Adam and Eve resulted in their spiritual separation from God (Genesis 3:8,21-24). And Satan will continue to deceive and wreak havoc on the seed of the woman and all humanity (Revelation 12:9; 20:2,3). Yet in the future, God promises a male descendant of the woman will crush and defeat Satan and his seed.

Is not this the gospel message? Didn't Jesus say He had come to give His life a ransom for many and to destroy the works of Satan (Matthew 20:28; John 12:31; 16:11), to proclaim release to the captives, to set free those who are downtrodden (Luke 4:18)? In other words, this text in Genesis 3 is already speaking of Jesus, the Savior, who would come to come to reverse the destructive works of Satan on all of humanity.

---

* There is also a reference to the conflict between the human followers of Satan or Christ who have either one or the other as their respective spiritual heads (Matthew 23:33; John 8:44; Galatians 3:26-29; Ephesians 4:15; 1 John 3:1,8; 5:19).

Was Genesis 3:15 Recognized
by the Jews as Messianic?

The answer is yes. The words themselves forced Jewish scholars to a Messianic application well before the birth of Christ.[12] This is why Dr. Charles Feinberg, Professor of Semitics and Old Testament at Talbot Seminary, has documented that, "There has never been a time, from ancient days to the present, when the Messianic interpretation of Genesis 3:15 has not had its able advocates."[13] The Jewish community in Alexandria (247 B.C.) and the later Targumim[14] prove this.[15]

In the Jewish community, the Targum Pseudo-Jonathan on Genesis 3:15 stands as proof that the ancient rabbis believed the words in this verse referred to "the days of the King, Messiah" (71:122). The same can be said for the Jerusalem Targum.[16]

In his *Exposition of Genesis*, the renowned Old Testament scholar H.C. Leupold observes that, "The Jewish church, according to the *Targum*, regarded this passage as Messianic from a very early day."[17]

5. Genesis 12:2,3; 22:18—Who is the seed of Abraham, Isaac, and Jacob that will eventually bless all nations?

The Biblical Texts (1400 B.C.)

> And Jehovah said to Abram... "I will make of you a great nation; I will bless you and make your name great, and you will be a blessing... and in you shall all families of the earth be blessed" (Genesis 12:2,3).
>
> And in your seed shall all the nations of the earth be blessed (Genesis 22:18).

The Context of These Passages

In Genesis 12, God has commanded Abram to leave his own country and travel to "the land I will show you" (Genesis 12:1, NASB). There God promises He will make him into a "great nation" and that the entire earth will be blessed through him. In Genesis 22, Abram (who is now Abraham because God changed his name) has been tested by God. Abraham showed God he is willing to do anything God asks. God sees this and promises Abraham that from *his seed* all the nations of the earth shall be blessed.

The Explanation of These Texts

According to the prophecy in Genesis 12, we know from history that it was literally fulfilled because: 1) God made Abraham into a great nation—the Jewish nation; 2) God did bless Abraham abundantly; 3) God did make his name great (he is honored by Jews, Muslims, and Christians). We also know that all peoples on the earth were blessed through Abraham, both culturally and spiritually.

> In matters of banking and commerce and finance, the world owes Israel an immense debt. In matters of statesmanship, particularly international states-manship, the debt is also large. From the time of David until now, Israelitish public men have been at the helm, sometimes in one nation and sometimes in another. In science and literature and music, the debt is likewise great. But high above all these things, the literature of Israel's prophets has been translated into all languages. Israel has been made the channel for communicating to mankind the monotheism of the religion of Yahweh. . . . Suppose we stop at this point, and ask: Has the promise been kept? Have all the families of the ground been blessed in Abraham and his seed? Who can answer otherwise than in the affirmative?[18]

In Genesis 22:18, God promises Abraham that all peoples on the earth will be blessed because of his *seed* (singular, referring to Messiah, see Galatians 3:16). It is likely that Abraham knew of the promise made by God to Adam and Eve that from the woman's seed a male descendant would come and crush Satan's head. Now God extends His promise through Abraham's seed. The question is, "Who is the offspring of Abraham God is speaking of who will bless all nations?"

At this point, it is too early to identify the specific person in the future who will bless all nations. But whoever the specific person or seed will be, he *must* be descended from this one man, Abraham.

The apostle Matthew places at the front of his book this important statement, "A record of the genealogy of Jesus Christ the son of David, the son of Abraham" (Matthew 1:1, NIV). Why? Because Matthew had read the Hebrew Scriptures and knew God had promised to bless all the nations through Abraham's seed. For Matthew, Jesus was the one God described to Abraham. The facts clearly show that no man has had such a spiritual influence on the world as Jesus Christ.[19] The spiritual blessing of Abraham is also evident to the apostle Paul who writes in Galatians 3:8,9: "The Scripture foresaw that God would justify the Gentiles by faith [in the Messiah], and announced the gospel in advance to Abraham: 'All nations will be blessed through you [Abraham's seed].' So those who have faith are blessed along with Abraham, the man of faith" (NIV).

Because of space limitations, we cannot describe in detail the increasingly narrow parental line God revealed. However, a brief outline of the scriptural promises reveals that God's special person could only come out of the following lineage and circumstances:

- from the seed of the woman (any possible man).
- from Abraham (one man's descendants are selected from all men on earth).
- from Isaac (not Ishmael: one-half of Abraham's lineage is eliminated—Genesis 26:2-4).
- from Jacob (not Esau: one-half of Isaac's lineage is now eliminated—Genesis 28:13,14).
- from Jesse (Isaiah 11:1; Luke 3:23,32).
- from David (Jesse had at least eight sons; seven are now eliminated—1 Samuel 16:10-13).
- from Bethlehem (all cities in the world are now eliminated but one—Micah 5:2).

6. Deuteronomy 18:15—Who is the "prophet like Moses" of whom God says, "You must listen to him"?

The Biblical Text (1400 B.C.)

[Moses is speaking] The Lord your God will raise up for you a prophet from among your own people, like myself; him you shall heed.... [God is speaking] I will raise up a prophet for them from among their own people, like yourself; I will put My words in his mouth and he will speak to them all that I command him; and if anybody fails to heed the words he speaks in My name, I Myself will call him to account (Deuteronomy 18:15,18,19)—The Torah.[20]

The Context of This Passage

Through Moses, God is warning Israel to remain separate from the evil practices of the surrounding Caananite nations (Deuteronomy 18:9-12). In His warning, God instructs Israel how to tell the difference between a "true prophet" and a "false prophet" (Deuteronomy 13:1-5; 18:19-22). Any prophet who speaks in the name of the Lord whose words do not come true is a "false prophet"; God has not spoken through him. In the same context God tells Israel He will send prophets who will truthfully speak for Him. What's more, Israel can someday expect a prophet who will be "like Moses," that God will specially raise up and identify.

The Explanation of the Text

Think for a moment. Would a "prophet like Moses" be a unique personage in Israel? Why would this "prophet like Moses" be considered a reference to the coming Messiah? First, it is a fact that throughout its history, the nation of Israel did *not* apply to *any* prophet these particular words. That is not to say that one or two individual rabbis did not try to make the application to a favored prophet. But it cannot be denied that the nation of Israel as a whole never acknowledged any Old Testament prophet to be "like Moses."[21]

Second, this was not a reference to Joshua because 1) there is no resemblance between Moses and Joshua; 2) Joshua is never said to be a prophet nor does he fulfill the office of a prophet; 3) it was specifically stated in Joshua's own time "no prophet has risen in Israel like Moses" (Deuteronomy 34:10, NASB).

Third, the word *prophet* is in the singular, so it must refer to some individual prophet in the future. Fourth, until Jesus came, no one was superior to Moses, for it was only said of Moses and Jesus that they knew the Lord and spoke to Him "face to face" (Deuteronomy 34:10; cf. Numbers 12:8; Matthew 3:17; Mark 9:7; John 11:41,42; 17:1-5).

Fourth, up to the time of Christ, it can be documented that the Jews had not believed that "the prophet" had yet arrived. Thus the leaders of Israel asked John the Baptist, "Are you the Prophet?" (John 1:21, NIV), which John denied. But when the people saw Jesus' miracles they said, "Surely this is the Prophet who is to come into the world" and "Surely this man is the Prophet" and "We have found the one Moses wrote about" (John 6:14; 7:40; 1:45, NIV).

What was the evidence that persuaded the people in Jesus' own time that He was the unique prophet God said was "like unto Moses"? Could anyone but the Messiah be worthy of being considered the one who is "like Moses"? In the following material we will supply parallels between Moses and Jesus, proving that Jesus was "like Moses." But we will also prove that Jesus was much greater than Moses. Only Jesus completely fulfilled and went beyond Moses' prophetic office and is the unique one God promised would come.

A. A great founder of religion. Moses gave God's revelation of the law and founded the religion of Israel. But Jesus gave God's complete revelation of grace and truth (John 1:17), fulfilled all the law (Matthew 5:17), and became the founder and Savior of the Christian religion (1 Timothy 2:5,6).

B. A great revealer of God. Moses revealed God in writing the Torah. Moses did not point people to himself, but faithfully wrote about God and about the one in the future whom God told him about. But Jesus claimed, "For if you believed *Moses,* you would believe Me; *for he wrote of Me.* But if you do not believe his writings, how will you believe My words?" (John 5:46,47, NASB, emphasis added). Yet Jesus just didn't speak about God; Jesus claimed He *was* God (John 5:18; 10:30).

C. A great law-giver. Moses was the only one authorized by God to give laws to Israel. But it was Jesus who gave God's full understanding of the law and gave "new" laws to Israel. Jesus quoted the law when He said, "You have heard that it was said..." but added what no other prophet had ever dared speak: "but I say unto you..." (Matthew 5:21,22). That's why "when Jesus had finished saying these things, the crowds were amazed at his teaching, because he taught as one who had authority, and not as their teachers of the law" (Matthew 7:28,29, NIV).

D. A great worker of miracles. Moses was a great worker of miracles (the ten plagues on Egypt; the parting of the Red Sea, etc.) (Exodus 7–14; Deuteronomy 34:10-12). But Jesus did even greater miracles than Moses. He said, "If I had not done among them what no one else did [his miracles], they would not be guilty of sin" (John 15:24, NIV).

In fact, no one could deny His miracles because they had been witnessed by literally thousands of people: "Men of Israel, listen to these words: Jesus the Nazarene, a man attested to you by God with miracles and wonders and signs which God performed through Him in your midst, just as *you yourself know...*" (Acts 2:22, NASB, emphasis added). Jesus not only commanded violent storms which obeyed Him, He instantly healed thousands of people from incurable illnesses and deformities, raised the dead, gave sight to those blind from birth, expelled demons, and even conquered death when He was resurrected from the dead (Matthew 4:23; 8:3,16,23-27; 9:6,35; 14:14,25; 15:30; 19:2; 21:14; Mark 1:34; 3:10; Luke 4:33-35,40; 7:11-15,21; 8:41-56; John 9:1-7; John 2:19-22; Acts 10:38). All this is why the multitudes were "completely astounded" (Mark 5:42, NASB) and they "marveled," saying, "Nothing like this was ever seen in Israel" (Matthew 9:33, NASB).

E. A great redeemer. Moses rescued Israel from the bondage and slavery of Egypt (Exodus 3–4; Acts 7:20-39). But Christ rescued the world from the bondage and slavery of sin (Matthew 20:28; Ephesians 2:1-8; Romans 3:28–4:6).

F. A great mediator. Moses was the mediator between God and Israel. But Jesus is now the Mediator between God and all humanity. First Timothy 2:5,6 says, "For there is one God and one mediator between God and men, the man Christ Jesus, who gave himself as a ransom for all men" (NIV).

G. A great intercessor. Moses was the great intercessor for Israel, preventing God from utterly destroying them when they worshiped the golden calf (Exodus 32:7-14; Numbers 14:11-20). But Jesus is a greater intercessor. He now intercedes on behalf of all mankind (John 3:16; Hebrews 7:25; note Numbers 21:4-9 and John 3:14).

H. A great prophet, judge, and king. Moses was a great prophet, judge, and king (Exodus 18:13; Deuteronomy 33:5). But Jesus was a greater prophet, judge, and king (John 1:19-21,29-34,45; Matthew 2:2; John 5:26-29; Hebrews 7:17).

I. Moses was like the Messiah. But Jesus was the Messiah. He told this to the common people and to those in authority, such as the Jewish high priest. "The woman said, 'I know that Messiah' (called Christ) 'is coming. When he comes, he will explain everything to us.' Then Jesus declared, *'I who speak to you am He'*" (John 4:25,26, NIV, emphasis added). The high priest asked Jesus, "Are you the Messiah?" Jesus replied, "I am" (Mark 14:61,62).

Was Deuteronomy 18:15 Recognized by the Jews as Messianic?

The Mishna, "Sefer ha-Mitzvot" in the Negative Commandments (number 13) states, "The prophet whom God will raise up must be 'from among your own people' (Deuteronomy 18:15). This means also that He must arise in the land of Israel."[22]

"The Talmud asserts 'that Messiah must be the greatest of future prophets, as being nearest in spirit to our master Moses.' This prediction [in Deuteronomy 18:15], then, could only receive its accomplishment in the Messiah. It was so understood by the Jews in the days of our Lord."[23]

7. Psalm 22—Who is the one crucified?

The Biblical Text (1000 B.C.)

> My God, my God, why have you forsaken me?... All who see me mock me; they hurl insults, shaking their heads: "He trusts in the LORD; let the LORD rescue him. Let him deliver him, since he delights in him."... I am poured out like water, and all my bones are out of joint. My heart has turned to wax; it has melted away within me. My strength is dried up like a potsherd, and my tongue sticks to the roof of my mouth; you lay me in the dust of death. Dogs have surrounded me; a band of evil men has encircled me, they have pierced my hands and my feet. I can count all my bones; people stare and gloat over me. They divide my garments among them and cast lots for my clothing (Psalm 22:1,7,8,14-18, NIV).

The Context of This Passage

Psalm 22 is both a cry of anguish and a song of praise to God. The New International Version properly identifies the context of this passage as "the anguished prayer of David as a godly sufferer victimized by the vicious and prolonged attacks of enemies whom he has not provoked and from whom the Lord has not (yet) delivered him."[24] The Hebrew scholar Charles Briggs explains the following about Psalm 22 in his book *Messianic Prophecy*:

> Psalm 22 describes a sufferer with stretched body, feverish frame and pierced hands and feet. He is surrounded by cruel enemies, who mock him for his trust in God, and divide his garments as their spoil. He is abandoned by God for a season, until he is brought to the dust of death. He is then delivered, and praises his deliverer with sacrifices.[25]

The Explanation of the Text

In this passage which describes the feelings and circumstances of King David, we find astonishing parallels that fit the future experience of Jesus Christ on the cross. The question is, then, are these parallels fiction, found only in the minds of Christians, or words that David wrote a thousand years before Christ which perfectly fit and predict the person of Jesus Christ?

As Baron has observed: "Are Christians right in interpreting this Psalm as a prediction of Christ? . . . It is the only interpretation which accords with common sense."[26] The following is an explanation of the actual words in the Psalm and a look at the incredibly accurate picture they paint of Jesus Christ during His crucifixion *one thousand years later*.

> 1. David said, "My God, my God, why have you forsaken me?" (Psalm 22:1).

Jesus said these exact words while dying on the cross (Matthew 27:46). They accurately expressed His grief as He bore the penalty for the sins of the entire world (1 Peter 2:24; 1 John 2:2). In other words, having the sins of all humanity placed to His account resulted in His temporary separation from God, His Father (Galatians 3:13,14).

> 2. David said, "All who see me mock me; they hurl insults, shaking their heads" (Psalm 22:7). The meaning of the word "shake" is "to shake or wag the head in mockery."[27] It is also a gesture of scorn and includes the fact that the adversaries were not only giving assent and approval to the victim's suffering, but also enjoyed seeing his adversities and calamities.[28]

All this happened to Jesus. He was literally scorned, despised and mocked by the crowds surrounding Him on the cross. The words David used, "They hurl insults, shaking their heads," perfectly fit: 1) the religious rulers who stood watching ("the rulers even sneered at him" [Luke 23:35, NIV]); 2) the soldiers ("the soldiers also came up and mocked him" [Luke 23:36-38, NIV]); and 3) one of the two criminals crucified next to Him ("one of the criminals who hung there hurled insults at him: 'Aren't you the Christ [Messiah]?'" [Luke 23:39, NIV]). Leading up to His crucifixion, Herod and his soldiers also mocked Him ("then Herod and his soldiers ridiculed and mocked him" [Luke 23:11, NIV]). At His trials the chief priests and the teachers of the law did the same ("the chief priests and the teachers of the law were standing there, vehemently accusing him" [Luke 23:10, NIV]). Finally, Matthew records the following about the crowd:

"Those who passed by hurled insults at him, shaking their heads.... 'Come down from the cross, if you are the Son of God'" [Matthew 27:39,40, NIV]. Again, all this fits the prophecy of Psalm 22.

> 3. *David said, "I am poured out like water, and all my bones are out of joint. My heart has turned to wax; it has melted away within me. My strength is dried up like a potsherd" (Psalm 22:14,15, NIV).*

Like water, Jesus' blood on the cross "poured out" of His body. Also, it is a fact that crucifixion pulls the bones and the body out of joint. This is what happened to Jesus. Finally, Jesus' strength dried up. He thirsted and then He died (John 19:28-30).

When blood *and* water came forth from Jesus' pierced side (John 19:34), this was medical proof that His heart had literally burst, fulfilling David's words, "My heart has turned to wax; it has melted away within me" (Psalm 22:14, niv).[29]

> 4. *David said, "Dogs have surrounded me; a band of evil men has encircled me, they have pierced my hands and my feet" (Psalm 22:16).*

Jesus was also encircled by people who hated Him, mocked Him, and were glad to watch Him suffer and die. Just as David said, they pierced His hands and His feet when they nailed Him to the cross (John 19:15-18).

> 5. *David said, "I can count all my bones; people stare and gloat over me. They divide my garments among them and cast lots for my clothing" (Psalm 22:17,18).*

While dying on the cross, Jesus looked down on the soldiers who had crucified Him and watched them gamble for His garments. For those who state that Jesus and the Gospel writers planned and acted out the prophecies of David, they must answer how Jesus motivated and arranged for the soldiers to do this. Also, how did He keep the soldiers from breaking His bones, a common Roman practice? Jesus was the only one of the three who were crucified whose legs were not broken (see Psalm 34:20). Further, He was the only one who suffered an unusual spear thrust into

His side (fulfilling Zechariah 12:10) which also did not break a bone (John 19:31-37).

Was Psalm 22 Recognized by the Jews as Messianic?

Few rabbis have accepted this passage as Messianic because of the dislike for a *suffering* and *crucified* Messiah. But the rabbinical writing called the *Pesikta Rabbat* (Piska 36:1-2), compiled in the ninth century A.D. (at the latest), although using much earlier material, refers to part of this passage as having reference to certain persons' sins that will weigh Messiah down under a yoke of iron. Thus, it says, "The Messiah's body is bent low" with great suffering.[30]

In addition, the great Hebrew scholar Edersheim observes that a remarkable comment appears in Yalkut* on Isaiah 60 which applies this passage in Psalm 22 to the Messiah, and uses almost the same words as the Gospel evangelists who describe the mocking behavior of the crowds surrounding the cross.[31]

As the late professor Charles Briggs of Union Theological Seminary, the man whose name appears on the official Hebrew Lexicon of the Hebrew Scriptures,[32] stated:

> These sufferings [of Psalm 22] transcend those of any historical sufferer, with the single exception of Jesus Christ. They find their exact counterpart in the sufferings of the cross.... This ideal is a Messianic ideal, and finds its only historical realization in Jesus Christ.[33]

But most Jewish people have rejected the idea of a suffering Messiah, in spite of this passage and Isaiah 53 (see Question #9). For example, David Baron, who had a strict rabbinical education, initially dismissed as absurd the idea that the Messiah should ever suffer. But he eventually changed his mind. Thorough study of the Hebrew Scriptures taught him the absolute need for forgiveness of sins[34] and brought him to the conclusion that the Scriptures did predict the Messiah would suffer for our sins. This led him to accept Jesus as the Messiah because "Jesus of Nazareth is the only individual in the [entire] history of the Jewish nation in whom all these [prophetic] characteristics are to be found."[35]

---

* Yalkut is the name given to the well-known collection of many older, accredited explanations and interpretations of the Hebrew testament.

8. Isaiah 9:6,7—Who is the child that is God and will have an everlasting kingdom?

The Biblical Text (700 B.C.)

For to us a child is born, to us a son is given, and the government will be on his shoulders. And he will be called Wonderful Counselor, *Mighty God*, Everlasting Father, Prince of Peace. Of the increase of his government and peace there will be no end. He will reign on David's throne and over his kingdom, establishing and upholding it with justice and righteousness from that time on and forever. The zeal of the LORD Almighty will accomplish this (Isaiah 9:6,7, NIV, emphasis added).

The Context of This Passage

Israel had been invaded by the Assyrian King Tiglath-Pileser (the first Jewish captivity) and as a result, the captured Israelites are plunged into despair and humiliation. In this prophecy God offers them hope for the future. He speaks of a coming light who will illuminate those who are in distress and darkness: "The people walking in darkness have seen a great light; on those living in the land of the shadow of death a light has dawned" (Isaiah 9:2, NIV).

Isaiah the prophet records that in the past God had humbled the land of Zebulun and the land of Naphtali (Northern and Southern Galilee). However, in the future God "will honor Galilee" (Isaiah 9:1, NIV). It is these people who, walking in darkness, will "see a great light."

Then God proceeds to describe the child who is to be born, the son who is to be given. He will be both human ("a child is born to us") and God ("he will be called ... Mighty God"), and thus, he will reign *forever* on David's throne. This can be no one other than the promised Messiah.

The Explanation of the Text

What this prophecy makes clear is the following:

1. A child will be born to the Jewish people.
2. The government will be upon His shoulders—He will be a ruling king.
3. He is called "Wonderful Counselor," "Mighty God," "Everlasting Father," "Prince of Peace"—as Old Testament scholar Dr. Merrill Unger points out, the phrase "his name" is a Hebrew idiom, and

means that the child would not actually bear the names, but "deserve them, and that they are appellatives or descriptive designations of his person and work."[36]

4. There would be no end to the increase of the child's government and peace.
5. He would reign on David's throne and over his kingdom for eternity.
6. The passage specifically places the fulfillment of this prophecy in Galilee since God says He will honor "Galilee of the Gentiles, by way of the sea, along the Jordan."

Concerning Zebulun and Naphtali, Hebrew scholar Edward J. Young comments, "This...district, despised even in New Testament times, was glorified when God honored it, and the fulfillment of the prophecy occurred when Jesus Christ the Son of God dwelt [settled] in Capernaum ['in the region of Zebulun and Naphtali'— Matthew 4:13]."[37]

Here in Isaiah 9:6 we have the clearest statement that the Messiah will be both God and man: He is called "Eternal Father" and "Mighty God" (*El Gibbor*)—the latter name is used of God Himself in Isaiah 10:21 and other passages. Noted Old Testament scholar E.J. Young has shown that the use of *El* in Isaiah "is found as a designation of God and only of him. . . . [Thus we see that] the Lord, the Holy One of Israel—and *El Gibbor* [the term used of the Son in Isaiah 9:6], are one and the same."[38]

Some scholars have noted the connection of this passage to Psalm 2, which not only speaks of the Lord's Messiah (verse 2), but also incredibly speaks of God as having a literal Son: "Do homage to the Son. . . . How blessed are all who take refuge in Him" (Psalm 2:12, NASB). Thus, they have noted, "The Messiah early became known not only as the son of David but also as the Son of God. 'Thou art my Son, this day have I begotten thee' (Psalm 2:7b). . . ."[39]

Was Isaiah 9:6,7 Recognized by the Jews as Messianic?

There can be no doubt that Jewish rabbis have accepted these verses as clearly applying to the Messiah. The Targum of Isaiah rendered this passage, "His name has been called from of old, Wonderful Counselor, Mighty God, He who lives forever, the Anointed One (or Messiah), in whose days peace shall increase upon us."[40]

Nineteenth-century theologian and professor of biblical criticism at the University of Aberdeen Paton J. Gloag observed that, "The ancient Jews refer these words *only* to the Messiah. 'The prophet,' says the Targum of Jonathan, 'speaketh of the house of David, because a child is born to us, a son is given to us . . . his name is called of old Wonderful in counsel, *God the mighty*, He who abideth forever, *the Messiah* whose peace shall be abundant upon us in His days.'"[41]

9. Isaiah 53—Who was crushed and pierced for our transgressions so that we would be healed by his wounds; upon whom did the Lord lay the iniquity of all mankind?

The Biblical Text (700 B.C.)

> Who has believed our message and to whom has the arm of the LORD been revealed? He grew up before him like a tender shoot, and like a root out of dry ground. He had no beauty or majesty to attract us to him, nothing in his appearance that we should desire him. He was despised and rejected by men, a man of sorrows, and familiar with suffering. Like one from whom men hide their faces he was despised, and we esteemed him not. Surely he took up our infirmities and carried our sorrows, yet we considered him stricken by God, smitten by him, and afflicted. But he was pierced for our transgressions, he was crushed for our iniquities; the punishment that brought us peace was upon him, and by his wounds we are healed. We all, like sheep, have gone astray, each of us has turned to his own way; and the LORD has laid on him the iniquity of us all (Isaiah 53:1-6, NIV).

The Context of This Passage

This passage is about the "Servant of the Lord." We find that the "Servant of the Lord" is a future individual whom Isaiah describes in what are called his "Servant Song" passages. Most agree that the passages devoted to describing the Servant are Isaiah 42:1-7; 49:1-7; 50:4-10; and 52:13–53:12.

The Explanation of the Text

In these four passages, we discover "the Servant" is the Messiah.

The texts themselves prove this, for "the Servant" is "the chosen One in whom Jehovah delights" (Isaiah 42:1); His mission is to bring the nation of Israel back to Jehovah (Isaiah 49:5); and He is to be "a light to the Gentiles"—in other words, to all the nations of the earth (Isaiah 42:1,6, NIV). This Servant cannot be Israel as some have claimed because "the Servant" is specifically described as one who has not been rebellious (Isaiah 50:5). We know from Israelite history that this description does not apply to the nation.

Isaiah 52:13–53:12 is the longest of the four Servant passages. Significantly, the passage is quoted and applied to Jesus Christ more frequently by New Testament writers than any other single passage in the Hebrew Scriptures.

In the text itself, Jehovah God calls this individual "*My servant*" (Isaiah 52:13), and states His Servant will ultimately be successful: "He will be raised and lifted up and greatly exalted" (Isaiah 52:13, NIV). Significantly, in the Hebrew these are the *same* words used by Isaiah to describe *the Lord* (Jehovah of Hosts) in Isaiah 6:1,3.

But look at verses 14 and 15. It is important to note that it doesn't seem as if the Servant is really to be successful at all. At the first appearance of the Servant, God informs us, many will be appalled at him since His appearance is disfigured, marred, and almost beyond human likeness (Isaiah 52:14). But then, very mysteriously and quickly, the picture changes. The text says, "*Just as there were many* who were appalled at him [the first picture]... *so will many* nations shut their mouths at Him" when they see Him the next time (Isaiah 52:14,15, emphasis added).

Is it logical to conclude that verse 14 is referring to Jesus Christ's first coming, when He is smitten, bruised, and beaten? And that verse 15 refers to His second coming, when He will return as the triumphant Messiah who rules the earth in power?

Dr. Walter Kaiser, Professor of Old Testament and Semitic languages at Trinity Evangelical Divinity School in Deerfield, Illinois, has correctly pointed out that according to the text "men would reject the Servant's message (53:1), His person (verse 2), and His mission (verse 3). But His vicarious suffering would effect an atonement between God and man (verses 4-6); and though He would submit to suffering (verse 7), death (verse 8), and burial (verse 9), He would subsequently be raised to life, exalted and richly rewarded (verses 10-12)."[42]

Who could Isaiah's Servant be? Who else but Jesus Christ ever 1) claimed He was the Messiah (Matthew

26:63-65; John 4:25,26); 2) claimed His blood was poured out for many for the forgiveness of sins (Matthew 26:28, cf. Isaiah 53:12); and 3) as He predicted, rose again from the grave (Matthew 17:22,23; Luke 24:45,46, cf. Isaiah 53:10, 11) to validate His claims?

Some have argued that the Servant who suffers in Isaiah 52 and 53 is actually Isaiah the prophet himself. They say Isaiah is using figurative language just like Jeremiah, who described his sufferings as a prophet when he said, "I am like a sheep led to the slaughter" (Jeremiah 11:19).

A second interpretation is that the suffering Servant stands for the nation of Israel. Israel has suffered tremendously throughout her history and possibly Isaiah speaks figuratively of the nation as the expiatory lamb for mankind. Some think Isaiah is saying that God has placed upon Israel the full impact of all mankind's sins so that all humanity can survive.[43]

But there are solid reasons why these two interpretations should be rejected. First, the biblical text itself teaches us the suffering Servant could *not* be Isaiah or the nation of Israel. The reason for this is found in verse 9 where we are told the Servant "had done *no* violence, nor was *any* deceit found in his mouth." This couldn't be Isaiah or the nation of Israel. Isaiah himself clearly states, "*I am a man* of unclean lips, and *I live among a people* of unclean lips" (Isaiah 6:5, NIV, emphasis added).

In another place Isaiah confesses, "Our offenses are many in your sight, and our sins testify against us" (Isaiah 59:12, NIV). So the biblical text itself proves neither Isaiah nor Israel fits the description of the suffering Servant who had "done no violence, nor was any deceit found in his mouth" (verse 9).

There is another reason why this passage must be a description of the coming Messiah and *cannot* be referring to either Isaiah or the nation of Israel. That reason is found in verse 10. There we learn that the suffering Servant gives his life as a "guilt offering," a "trespass offering."

According to the Hebrew Scriptures, a trespass offering *must* be a lamb without blemish; it *must* be perfect (Leviticus 6:6,7). The life that's given in atonement for others must be a perfect life. Here again, Isaiah the prophet admits neither he nor the nation of Israel qualifies.

Finally, proof that Isaiah is speaking of the coming Messiah and not the nation of Israel is found in Isaiah 53:8 where the text states, "For the transgression of my people he was stricken" (NIV). Who are the "my people" spoken about? This must be Israel. But if the "Servant" is stricken for the transgression of "my people," then the Servant can't be Israel. This must be the Messiah who will suffer.

Finally, throughout this passage, the Servant is portrayed as an individual. It speaks of what *he* has done; how *he* was despised; how *he* was rejected, and how the Lord laid on *him* the iniquity of us all. All of this the Servant did on behalf of "my people."

Is This Text Speaking of Jesus Christ?

In the material below we present ten parallels between what Isaiah says will happen to the Messiah and what the historical accounts in the Gospels say happened to Jesus. Remember, Isaiah is writing these words a full seven centuries before Christ was ever born.

1. *"But he was pierced for our transgressions"* (Isaiah 53:5, NIV).

   "And when they came to the place called the Skull, there they crucified him" (Luke 23:33, NIV; cf. John 19:34).

2. *"He was crushed for our iniquities; the punishment that brought us peace was upon him, and by his wounds we are healed"* (53:5, NIV).

   "And He Himself bore our sins in His body on the cross, that we might die to sin and live to righteousness; for by His wounds you were healed" (1 Peter 2:24, NASB).

3. *"We all, like sheep, have gone astray, each of us has turned to his own way; and the LORD has laid on him the iniquity of us all"* (53:6, NIV).

   "God was in Christ reconciling the world to Himself, not counting their trespasses against them" (2 Corinthians 5:19, NASB).
   Peter said about Jesus' death on the cross, "For Christ died for sins once for all, the righteous for the unrighteous, to bring you to God" (1 Peter 3:18, NIV); "For you were like sheep going astray" (1 Peter 2:25, NIV).

4. *"He was oppressed and afflicted, yet he did not open his mouth; he was led like a lamb to the slaughter, and as a sheep before her shearers is silent, so he did not open his mouth"* (53:7, NIV).

   "When he was accused by the chief priests and the elders, he gave no answer. Then Pilate asked him,

'Don't you hear the testimony they are bringing against you?' But Jesus made no reply, not even to a single charge—to the great amazement of the governor" (Matthew 27:12-14, NIV).

5. *"By oppression and judgment he was taken away"* (53:8, NIV).

"'Am I leading a rebellion,' said Jesus, 'that you have come out with swords and clubs to capture me? Every day I was with you, teaching in the temple courts, and you did not arrest me. But the Scriptures must be fulfilled.' Then everyone deserted him and fled.... The chief priests and the whole Sanhedrin were looking for evidence against Jesus so that they could put him to death, but they did not find any. Many testified falsely against him, but their statements did not agree.... They all condemned him as worthy of death. Then some began to spit at him; they blindfolded him, struck him with their fists, and said, 'Prophesy!' And the guards took him and beat him" (Mark 14:48-50,55,56,64,65, NIV).

6. *"For he was cut off from the land of the living; for the trangression of my people he was stricken"* (53:8, NIV).

"But you disowned the Holy and Righteous One, and...put to death the Prince of life.... For you first, God raised up His Servant" (Acts 3:14,15,26, NASB).

"For while we were still helpless, at the right time Christ died for the ungodly.... God demonstrates His own love toward us, in that while we were yet sinners, Christ died for us" (Romans 5:6,8, NASB).

7. *"He was assigned a grave with the wicked, and with the rich in his death, though he had done no violence, nor was any deceit in his mouth"* (53:9, NIV).

"Two robbers were crucified with Him" (Matthew 27:38, NASB).

"Summoning the centurion, he [Pilate] asked him if Jesus had already died. When he learned from the centurion that it was so, he gave the body to Joseph [of Arimathea, a man of wealth]. So Joseph bought some linen cloth, took down the body, wrapped it in the linen, and placed it in a tomb cut out of rock. Then he rolled a stone against the entrance of the tomb" (Mark 15:44-46, NIV).

8. *"Yet it was the LORD's will to crush him and cause him to suffer,... The LORD makes his life a guilt offering..."* (53:10, NIV).

"But the things which God announced beforehand by the mouth of all the prophets, that His Christ [Messiah] should suffer, He has thus fulfilled" (Acts 3:18, NASB).

"All this is from God...God was reconciling the world to himself in Christ" (2 Corinthians 5:18,19, NIV).

9. *"After the suffering of his soul, he will see the light of life and be satisfied; by his knowledge my righteous servant will justify many, and he will bear their iniquities"* (53:11, NIV).

"For I delivered to you as of first importance what I also received, that Christ died for our sins according to the Scriptures, and that He was buried, and that He was raised on the third day according to the Scriptures, and that He appeared to Cephas, then to the twelve. After that He appeared to more than five hundred brethren at one time" (1 Corinthians 15:3-6, NASB).

"...being justified as a gift by his grace through the redemption which is in Christ Jesus" (Romans 3:24, NASB).

10. *"...because he poured out his life unto death, and was numbered with the transgressors. For he bore the sin of many, and made intercession for the transgressors"* (53:12, NIV).

"Two robbers were crucified with him, one on his right and one on his left" (Matthew 27:38, NIV).

"Father, forgive them, for they do not know what they are doing" (Luke 23:34, NIV).

"He was delivered over to death for our sins and was raised to life for our justification" (Romans 4:25, NIV).

"Christ Jesus, who died—more than that, who was raised to life—is at the right hand of God and is also interceding for us" (Romans 8:34, NIV).

"Therefore he is able to save completely those who come to God through him, because he always lives to intercede for them" (Hebrews 7:25, NIV).

Are the above parallels difficult to explain on purely rationalistic grounds? As the Scottish exegete and theologian Paton J. Gloag, once professor of biblical criticism at the University of Aberdeen, argued:

> We do not see how anyone can read this remarkable prophecy without being struck with its pointed resemblance to the character, sufferings, and death of the Lord Jesus. The portrait is complete: the resemblance is striking and unmistakable. Indeed, it seems more like a history of the past than a prediction of the future: ... In no portion of Scripture, even in the most Evangelical parts of the New Testament, is the doctrine of the atonement, that grand characteristic of Christianity, so clearly stated.... And yet nothing is more indisputable than that these words were uttered centuries before our Lord came into this world.[44]

Was Isaiah 52:13–53:12 Recognized by Jews as Messianic?

Proof that this passage has long been acknowledged as Messianic can be seen from the fact that the early rabbis developed the idea of two Messiahs from this passage. Although they could not reconcile the statements that so clearly spoke of a suffering and dying Messiah with those verses in other passages that spoke of an eternally triumphant and victorious Messiah, it is important to note the early rabbis did recognize that *both* pictures somehow applied to the Messiah. But rather than seeing one Messiah in two different roles, they saw two Messiahs—the suffering and dying Messiah, called "Messiah ben Joseph," and the victorious conquering Messiah, called "Messiah ben David."

Today, many Orthodox Jews still wait for this political Messiah, Messiah ben David, who will conquer and rule forever. And interestingly, at the same time, there are some who accept Jesus Christ as the "other" Messiah, Messiah ben Joseph, even though they deny His deity.[45]

Dr. Raphael Patai, formerly of the University of Jerusalem, who has authored 20 books on subjects relating to Jewish religious beliefs, has observed the following, "When the death of the Messiah became an established tenet in Talmudic times, this was felt to be irreconcilable with the belief in the Messiah as the Redeemer who would usher in the blissful millennium of the Messianic age. The dilemma was solved by splitting the person of the Messiah in two...."[46] Thus, on the basis of Isaiah 53, the Babylonian Talmud boldly predicts, "Messiah ben Joseph will be slain...."[47]

The different views that orthodox rabbis have given to this passage throughout history can be found in *Rays of Messiah's Glory*. We'd like to point out that rabbis such as the great Maimonides and Rabbi Crispin thought it was *wrong* to apply Isaiah 53 to the nation of Israel. Rather, they thought this passage clearly described God's Messiah:

> ...the weight of Jewish authority preponderates in favor of the Messianic interpretation of this chapter.... That until recent times this prophecy has been almost universally received by Jews as referring to Messiah is evident from Targum [J]onathan, who introduces Messiah by name in chapter LII.13; from the Talmud ("Sanhedrin," fol. 98,b); and from the Zohar.... In fact, until Rashi [Rabbi Solomon Izaaki (1040–1105), considered the originator of the modern school of Jewish interpretation], who applied it to the Jewish nation, the Messianic interpretation of this chapter was almost universally adopted by Jews....[48]

The "father" of modern Hebrew, Wilhelm Gesenius, has also written, "'It was only the *later* Jews who abandoned this [Messianic] interpretation [of Isaiah 53], no doubt in consequence of their controversies with the Christians.'"[49]

In a debate with Dr. Walter Kaiser on the "John Ankerberg Show," Dr. Pinchas Lapide, one of only four orthodox Jewish scholars in the world who is also a New Testament scholar, stated: "I fully agree with Dr. Kaiser that Isaiah 53 lends itself in many startling similarities to the life, career and death of Jesus of Nazareth...."[50] Amazingly, Dr. Lapide even believes Jesus actually physically rose from the dead after being crucified because of the many compelling historical facts in its favor.[51] Yet Dr. Lapide concludes that Jesus is the Messiah for the Gentiles, and not for the Jews.

We have only one question: If Jesus Christ is not God's suffering Servant found in Isaiah 53, then who is?

10. Jeremiah 23:5,6—Who is the righteous Branch, the wise king, who will be called "the Lord our righteousness"?

The Biblical Text (600 B.C.)

> Behold, the days come, says Jehovah, that I will raise
> to David a righteous Branch, and He will reign as
> king and act wisely, and shall do justice and righ-
> teousness in the earth. In his days Judah shall be
> saved, and Israel shall dwell safely. And this is his
> name (by) which he shall be called, Jehovah our righ-
> teousness (Jeremiah 23:5,6).

The Context of This Passage

In Jeremiah 23 God has pronounced judgment on the
false leaders and prophets of Israel who were responsible for
scattering the people and driving them away from God
(Jeremiah 23:1,2; 23:9-27). We know from history and
Scripture this divine judgment was the Babylonian captivity and exile. God now declares He will gather the remnant
of His flock from all the countries and bring them back
where they will be fruitful and increase in number (Jeremiah 23:3,4).

It is at this point God states the amazing words about the
future found in verses 5 and 6.

The Explanation of the Text

Proof that this passage is speaking about the Messiah
can be seen from the following:

1. At least four other scriptural passages refer to a
   "Branch" who is acknowledged by many Jewish
   rabbis as being the Messiah (Jeremiah 33:15;
   Isaiah 4:2; Zechariah 3:8; 6:12,13). Many have
   agreed that "this term [the Branch] is one of the
   proper names of the Messiah."[52]

2. This person, the "Branch," is literally called "Jehovah our righteousness." This indicates that
   Messiah is somehow God (Jehovah). The Messiah
   is thus stated to be "our righteousness." What this
   means we will see in a moment.

But first, who would dare claim to be "the Branch"? Who
would dare utter he was "Jehovah"? Who would ever claim
to be "our righteousness"? There is only one person in
history who has claimed this—Jesus Christ.

What does this passage mean when it says this "Branch"
from David will be "Jehovah our righteousness"? We agree

with Lutheran scholar Dr. Theodore Laestch who, in his commentary on Jeremiah, has compared other Messianic promises and concluded:

> It is the righteousness which the Seed of David, who is the Woman's Seed of Genesis 3:15, procures for mankind by bruising Satan's head. As the Servant of the Lord, he bore the sins of man (Isaiah 53:11), which the Lord laid on him (verse 6) who had done no wrong (verse 9) and who suffered all the penalties man had deserved (verses 5-6). By his vicarious, substitutionary fulfillment of all the demands of the mandatory and punitive justice of God he became "our righteousness," establishing this righteousness as the norm to be followed in his kingdom. Since this righteousness was procured and established by him whom God calls "Jehovah our righteousness," it is a righteousness not only promised in the Old Testament, but as the righteousness procured by Jehovah it is as timeless as the Lord, retroactive (Hebrews 9:15)....[53]

Let us ask, Could all of this be true of anyone but Jesus Christ? In all of Jewish history only Jesus Christ stated that He would freely justify sinners before God, thereby granting them the privilege of eternal life (Matthew 20:28; John 3:16; 4:13,14; 5:21-29; 6:47). Further, in Romans 3:21-26 we discover that Jesus is the one who has become "our righteousness" according to the plan of Jehovah: "But now a righteousness *from God*, apart from law, has been made known, to which *the Law and the Prophets* testify. This righteousness from God comes through faith in *Jesus Christ* to all who believe" (Romans 3:21,22, NIV, emphasis added; see Philippians 3:9).

Was Jeremiah 23:5,6 Recognized by the Jews as Messianic?

The Targum of Isaiah reads, "I will raise up to David a righteous Messiah, a king who will reign wisely," proving the rabbis held this passage to be Messianic.[54] As other Messianic experts have stated: "There is scarcely any contrary opinion among ancient and also modern Jews but that this is a Messianic prophecy."[55]

The renowned Rabbi David Kimchi (1160–1235) was such a great scholar of the Hebrew Scriptures that the Jews had a saying about him: "No Kimchi, no understanding of the Scriptures."[56] And concerning this verse, Rabbi Kimchi wrote, "By the righteous Branch is meant Messiah."[57] Further, those who wrote Targum Jonathan agreed with Kimchi; they introduced the Messiah by name in this passage.[58]

In conclusion, this passage is clearly Messianic. It teaches the Messiah will be "Jehovah our righteousness" and in all of Israel's history, only Jesus Christ can be found who logically fits this description.

11. Daniel 9:24-27—Who is the "Anointed One" to be "cut off" after 483 years?

The Biblical Text (500 B.C.)

> Seventy "weeks" are decreed for your people and your holy city to finish transgression, to put an end to sin, to atone for wickedness, to bring in everlasting righteousness, to seal up vision and prophecy and to anoint the Most Holy. Know and understand this: from the issuing of the decree to restore and rebuild Jerusalem until the Anointed One, the Ruler, comes, there will be seven "weeks" and sixty-two "weeks." It will be rebuilt with streets and a trench, but in times of trouble. After the sixty-two "weeks," the Anointed One will be cut off and will have nothing. The people of the ruler who will come will destroy the city and the sanctuary (Daniel 9:24-26a).

The Context of This Passage

Daniel lived during the Babylonian captivity. He tells us he wrote this passage in the first year of the reign of King Darius, son of Xerxes (Daniel 9:1). From history we know that the reign of King Darius began in the year 538/537 B.C.

Daniel informed us that he was reading the Scriptures which had foretold both the Babylonian captivity and the return of the captive Israelites to their land. Thus, he says, "I, Daniel, understood from the Scriptures, according to the word of the LORD given to Jeremiah the prophet, that the desolation of Jerusalem would last seventy years" (Daniel 9:2, NIV).

Jeremiah also stated, "This whole land shall be a desolation and a horror and these nations shall serve the king of Babylon seventy years" (Jeremiah 25:11, NASB). At the end of this time, the Lord said, "When seventy years have been completed for Babylon, I will visit you and fulfill My good word to you, to bring you back to this place" (Jeremiah 29:10, NASB).

Daniel had been involved in the first deportation to Babylon in 605 B.C. when Nebuchadnezzar, son of Nabopolassar, the king of Babylon, had invaded Palestine. Now, in 538 B.C. (67 years later), Daniel realized from the prophecy of Jeremiah that the 70-year captivity was nearing its completion.

The Explanation of This Text

How do we know Gabriel's message to Daniel in this prophecy is about the Messiah? Because the Hebrew word that is used is *Mashiach* and must be translated "Messiah" or "the Anointed One."[59] As the great Princeton scholar, Professor R.D. Wilson (who was fluent in 45 languages and dialects), states, "Daniel IX, 25,26 is one of the two [Hebrew] passages where the expected Savior of Israel is called *Messiah*."[60]

Yet some have objected to this view, claiming that rather than speaking of the "Messiah," the "Anointed One," Daniel is instead referring to Cyrus, king of Persia. But this cannot apply to King Cyrus because, as we shall see, verses 25 and 26 declare that the "Messiah" will not arrive until some 400 years *after* Cyrus lived. In a similar manner, it cannot apply to the Syrian ruler Antiochus Epiphanes, since he died in 164 B.C. As we shall see, the prophecy talks about the "Messiah" coming to Jerusalem alive almost 200 years after that. Therefore, this one who is called *Mashiach Nagid*—Messiah the Prince—cannot refer to either Cyrus or to Antiochus Epiphanes. As Professor E.J. Young has said, "The non-Messianic interpretation is utterly inadequate."[61]

Who, then, is the Messiah who will come? Whoever the Messiah is, he will appear on the scene *after* the rebuilding of Jerusalem (Daniel 9:25,26) and be killed *before* Jerusalem and the temple are again destroyed.

In verses 25 and 26, the text states that once the decree is issued to restore and rebuild Jerusalem, the Messiah will come after 69 "weeks." Then, he will be "cut off and have nothing." The verb rendered "to cut off" has the meaning, "to destroy; to strike, to smite; to punish with death."[62] Leupold correctly states, "The verb used [here] (*karath*), . . . frequently refers to a form of violent death."[63]

And what is the meaning of the term "weeks"? For us today, the term "week" is restricted to mean a period of seven days. But the Hebrew word is not so restricted and instead stands for "units of seven." The Hebrew word used here is *shabuim*, the plural form of the word *shabua*, translated as "sevens" in the NIV and as "weeks" in the NASB. As we shall see, the context must determine what "units of seven" is meant—whether it refers to units of seven days, weeks, years, etc.

In context, Daniel 9:23-27 demands that the plural word *shabuim* must refer to units of seven *years*. Thus, Daniel would be speaking of 70 units, or periods of seven years, for a total of 490 years. (In our book *The Case for Jesus the Messiah*, we cite five reasons for this conclusion.)

In light of these facts, Harold W. Hoehner, author of *Chronological Aspects of the Life of Christ* agrees that "the term *shabuim* in Daniel 9 most reasonably refers to a unit of seven years. To make it anything else does not make good sense."[64]

According to this prophecy, the Messiah will appear at the end of the 69 weeks (the seven weeks [49 years] plus 62 weeks [434 years]) or a total of 483 years. After the 69 weeks (483 years) the destruction of the city and the temple will take place. (We know from history this took place in 70 A.D. under Titus and his Roman legions who destroyed Jerusalem.)

But from what year and what decree (the decree "to restore and rebuild Jerusalem") are we to begin to count the number of years until Messiah?

The prophecy cannot refer to the decree of Cyrus (539 B.C.), Tattenai (519/18 B.C.), or Artaxerxes (457 B.C.) because all these only refer to rebuilding the temple and not the *city* of Jerusalem which the prophecy demands. Only the decree given by Artaxerxes to Nehemiah in 444 B.C. involves a decree to rebuild *Jerusalem* (Nehemiah 2:1-8; cf. Hoehner, 126-128).

We are now ready to determine the date from the decree of Artaxerxes (444 B.C.) until after the 69th week (483 years later) when Gabriel announced the Messiah would be killed in Jerusalem. Using the accepted 360-day lunar year calendar, it turns out to be A.D. 33, the very time in which Jesus Christ lived and was crucified in Jerusalem![65]

The important point in this prophetic passage is this: Clearly, the Messiah had to come by the end of the 69th week—483 years after the issuing of the decree. Again, we stress that the time between the decree authorizing *Jerusalem* to be rebuilt (verse 25—444 B.C.) and the coming of the Messiah was to be 69 "sevens" or 483 years (7 + 62 units = 69 x 7 years). That is the exact time that Jesus Christ was alive and ministering. And since the prophecy restricts the appearance of the Messiah to this time period, there is simply no other logical candidate for the Messiah. Again, this prophecy proves that Jesus Christ is the *only* possible candidate to be the Jewish Messiah.

**Was Daniel 9:24-27 Recognized
by the Jews as Messianic?**

Since this text explicitly speaks of the Messiah it would
be difficult for any Jewish rabbi to deny it. Still, because
this prophecy predicted the Messiah was to be "cut off"
(die), some have denied that it referred to the Messiah.[66]

But to their credit, many rabbis have boldly stated this
passage predicts the specific time of the Messiah's appearing so exactly that it cannot be escaped. For example, Rabbi
Nehumias, who lived about 50 years *before* Christ, is cited
by Grotius as saying that the time fixed by Daniel for the
appearing of the Messiah could not go beyond the next 50
years.[67] This leads us to conclude that if Christ was *not* the
Messiah, then Israel had no Messiah. Again, if Messiah was
to come, it had to be at the exact same time period as that in
which Christ lived.

The Talmud advises, "In Daniel is delivered to us the end
of the Messiah [i.e., 'the time of His appearance and death'
—Rabbi Jarchi]."[68] This prophecy was so powerful that the
Talmud even records that around the time of Titus (A.D. 70)
it was believed that the Messiah *had* already come! But the
feeling was that Messiah's appearance had been concealed
from the Jews until they were rendered more worthy of His
appearance.[69]

**12. Micah 5:2—Who is the one who is eternal, who will
be the ruler over Israel, who is born in Bethlehem
Ephrathah?**

The Biblical Text (700 B.C.)

> But you Bethlehem Ephrathah, though you are least
> among the thousands of Judah, out of you He shall
> come forth to Me to be ruler in Israel, His goings forth
> have been from old, from the days of eternity (Micah
> 5:2).

The Context of This Passage

Micah begins with a statement of doom concerning a
siege laid against Israel and its ruler. It is immediately
followed by a statement of hope, the foretelling of a future
ruler of Israel, a "He" who will bring lasting security to
Israel and whose influence will extend "to the ends of the
earth" (verse 4).[70] Note that the prophecy is specific. It
identifies Bethlehem as "Ephrathah" (the older name for

Bethlehem—Genesis 35:16,19; 48:7; Ruth 1:2; 4:11) which distinguishes this Bethlehem from other towns named Bethlehem such as the one in Zebulun (Joshua 19:15). Use of the term "Ephrathah" also identifies Bethlehem as the town in which David was born (1 Samuel 17:12), further establishing the Messianic connection between the Messiah and King David's throne.[71]

The Explanation of the Text

Grammatically, the term *from old* must apply to the one who is ruler from the days of eternity.[72] This ruler's activities are said to stem from the ancient past, yet his coming is still future.

The term *from old* literally means from "ancient time, aforetime." Significantly, this word (*qedem*) is also used of God Himself in the Old Testament (e.g., Deuteronomy 33:27; Habakkuk 1:12). The words *from the days of eternity* (*mee mai-oulom*) literally mean from "ancient time or eternity." Thus, the word *old* and, in some translations, the phrase *ancient times* are both appropriate designations of eternity. For example, the Hebrew word for "ancient times" is also used in Micah 4:7 where it says, "And Jehovah shall reign over them . . . *forever*."

The fact that such terms were used of a future ruler indicates that Micah expected a supernatural figure. This harmonizes with Isaiah's expectation of the Messiah in Isaiah 9:6 where the future Messianic King is called "eternal" and "God" (*El*), again, a word Isaiah uses only of God.[73] In his *A Commentary on the Minor Prophets*, Homer Hailey points out that the words *from old, from ancient times* "indicate more than that He descends from an ancient lineage; it relates Him to God, the Eternal One. His rule reaches back into eternity."[74]

The meaning of this verse revolves around two key points:

1. Like his ancestor King David, this future ruler of Israel will be born in insignificant Bethlehem.

2. But somehow, his goings forth, his activities, extend back into eternity.

Here, the outstanding Lutheran scholar E.W. Hengstenberg reveals what Micah is saying, as the prophet writes seven centuries before Christ: "First, the existence of the Messiah before his birth in time, in Bethlehem, is pointed out in general; and *then*, in contrast with all time, it is vindicated to eternity. This could not fail to afford a great consolation to Israel. He who hereafter, in a visible manifestation, was to deliver them from their misery, was already in existence—during it, before it, and through all eternity."[75]

Thus, the one we have been emphasizing in this book, the one who literally fulfilled the previous ten prophecies, Jesus Christ was born in Bethlehem exactly 700 years later.

His ruling over Israel is to be yet future, at His return, as He Himself prophesied: "Jesus said to them, 'I tell you the truth, at the renewal of all things, when the Son of Man sits on his glorious throne, you who have followed me will also sit on twelve thrones, judging the twelve tribes of Israel'" (Matthew 19:28, NIV); and "When the Son of Man comes in his glory, and all the angels with him, he will sit on his throne in heavenly glory. All the nations will be gathered before him, and he will separate the people one from another as a shepherd separates the sheep from the goats" (Matthew 25:31,32, NIV; cf. Luke 19:11-15,27).

Was Micah 5:2 Recognized by the Jews as Messianic?

The book of Micah has long been acknowledged as Messianic:

> All the ancient Jewish interpreters adhere to the Messianic meaning.... So also the testimony of the Targums is in favor of the Messianic interpretation of the prophecy. Thus the Targum of Jonathan says: "And thou, Bethlehem of Ephrathah, little art thou to be reckoned among the thousands of the house of Judah; out of thee shall proceed in my presence the Messiah to exercise sovereignty over Israel; whose name has been called from eternity, from the days of the everlasting." "Thou art little," observes Rabbi Jarchi, "but out of thee shall come forth to me King Messiah."[76]

Edersheim states that among the rabbis, "The well-known passage, Micah 5:2, is admittedly Messianic. So [also] in the Targum ... and by later Rabbis."[77]

That the Jews recognized this as a Messianic prophecy is also evident from the fact that the priests and scribes of Herod's day knew that the Messiah would be born in Bethlehem on the basis of this prophecy (Matthew 2:5,6). Thus, the common Jewish belief at the time of Christ was that they "unanimously regarded this passage as containing a prophecy of the birth of the Messiah in Bethlehem."[78] This is proven not only by Matthew 2:5,6 but by John 7:42 as well.

13. Zechariah 12:10—Who is Jehovah, "the one they have pierced," for whom Jerusalem and all the nation of Israel will weep and mourn?

The Biblical Text (500 B.C.)

> And I will pour on the house of David, and on the inhabitants of Jerusalem, the spirit of grace and of prayers. And they shall look on *Me* whom they have pierced, and they shall mourn for *Him*, as one mourns for an only son, and they shall be bitter over Him, as one that is in bitterness over the firstborn (Zechariah 12:10, emphasis added).

The Context of This Passage

This text says that sometime in the future God will pour out His Spirit on Israel and bring them to a painful understanding of a crucial event that happened in the past. What will they understand? This is one of the most amazing statements given by God in Scripture. He says, "[They] will look *on me, the one they have pierced*, and they will mourn for *him* as one mourns for an only child..." (NIV, emphasis added). The question is, who is this one that Israel is yet to look upon and, because of what they see, will begin to mourn?

The Explanation of the Text

Zechariah is a key Messianic book for providing additional evidence that the Jewish Messiah was to be not just a man, but the incarnation of God Himself. "Perhaps in no other single book in the Old Testament scriptures is Messiah's Divinity so clearly taught as in Zechariah."[79] In Zechariah 2:10 the prophet has already emphasized the startling revelation that God Himself would live among the Jewish people: "'Shout and be glad, O Daughter of Zion. For *I am coming*, and *I will live among you*,' declares the LORD" (NIV, emphasis added).

Here, Zechariah is relating the words of Jehovah God, who says, "They will look on *Me* whom they have pierced."

Jehovah Himself claims to be the one Israel has pierced. But when did Israel ever pierce Jehovah?

Notice that in the middle of the statement, "They will look on *Me* whom they have pierced, and they shall mourn for *Him*," the pronouns are significantly changed. They refer to different persons. What was at first a reference to Jehovah now becomes a reference to an unidentified "Him" that the entire nation of Israel will mourn for. Again, *two* specific persons are spoken of: 1) the Lord who is pierced and 2) an unknown *Him* who will be mourned over as an only Son. Delitzsch and Gloag comment:

> Some endeavor to escape the Messianic application of the prediction by supposing that the word "pierced" is to be taken in a metaphorical sense.... But it is doubtful if the word can be taken in this ... sense; it denotes "to thrust through," "to pierce as with a spear." Besides, the mourning here is expressed as the mourning for the dead: One "mourning for his only son, and in bitterness for his first born."[80]

This passage certainly raises some important questions. If the Hebrew word for "to pierce," is "to thrust through, to slay by death,"[81] then when did Israel ever *slay* Jehovah? And how could the Creator of heaven and the earth be slain by men? It would seem that this passage, like Isaiah 9:6, Micah 5:2, and others, can only be explained through an incarnation of God Himself: Messiah would be both God and man.

Thus, Zechariah says Israel will someday realize they have actually killed Jehovah their God, and will therefore begin a great and bitter mourning over Him, just as a family would mourn over the death of their only son who is greatly beloved.

And this prophecy only fits Jesus Christ. Why? Jesus Christ is the only one in all Israelite history who ever 1) claimed to be God, 2) claimed to be the Messiah, and 3) was actually crucified and killed by the inhabitants of Jerusalem.

Thus, the Jews in the New Testament recognized that only Jesus fit the words of this prophecy. The apostle John wrote, "In the beginning was the Word, and the Word was with God, and the Word was God.... And the Word became flesh, and dwelt among us, and we beheld His glory, glory as of the only begotten from the Father, full of grace and truth" (John 1:1,14, NASB). Jesus Christ was the very incarnation of God.

The apostle Paul believed Jesus was God and that He volunteered to die for our sins. Paul taught that Jesus was the one, "Who, being in very nature God ... made himself nothing, taking the very nature of a servant. ... And being found in appearance as a man, he humbled himself and became obedient to death—even death on a cross!" (Philippians 2:6-8, NIV).

Finally, it says that the entire nation will mourn and grieve bitterly over the death of this one who has been pierced, "as one mourns for an only child." Would the Jewish people mourn for this one as for the death of their only son, if He wasn't actually one of their Jewish sons—as Jesus Christ was?

What if the Jewish people someday come to recognize that Jesus really was their Messiah? What if they come to understand who He really is? What if they someday look upon Him as God, "the one whom they have pierced"? Wouldn't Zechariah's prophecy be fulfilled? Wouldn't there be tremendous weeping in Jerusalem?

Remember, God pours out His Spirit on His people so people will come to know His true Messiah, who loved them so much He gave His life (was pierced through) for them. As Isaiah said, "The LORD has laid on him the iniquity of us all" (Isaiah 53:6, NIV).

Was Zechariah 12:10 Recognized by the Jews as Messianic?

That this prophecy refers to the Messiah was admitted by the rabbis.[82] For example, this prophecy "is applied to the Messiah the Son of Joseph in the Talmud (Sukk.52a) and so is verse 12. ..."[83] Here we see that some interpreters, trying to avoid the clear implication of the words, have attempted to apply this passage to the "other" Messiah who would suffer, Messiah Ben Joseph.

> ... the later interpreters explaining it of Messiah Ben Joseph, or the suffering Messiah, whom they invented to meet the passages of Scripture that speak so clearly of this characteristic of the promised Redeemer. But as they believed that this Messiah son of Joseph was a mere man, the difficulty met them that Jehovah declared "they shall look on ME whom they have pierced"; so that if it refers to the Messiah he cannot be a mere man, but must be divine.[84]

In spite of this, we stress again that when Jehovah says "they will look on me, the one they have pierced," this prophecy uniquely fits only Jesus Christ in all of human history.

Conclusion: Who Is the Messiah?

After carefully examining several prophecies, we see that Jesus Christ has fulfilled all of them. No one else in all human history has ever done so.

And we have examined just a few of the prophecies concerning the Messiah. Had we space, there are dozens of others which we could have discussed that are just as specific as these. For example,

1. He will be born of a virgin (Isaiah 7:14; see Matthew 1:23).
2. He would live in Nazareth of Galilee (Isaiah 9:1,2; see Matthew 2:23; 4:15,16).
3. His birth would occasion the massacre of Bethlehem's children (Jeremiah 31:15; see Matthew 2:18).
4. His mission would include the Gentiles (Isaiah 42:1-3,6; see Matthew 12:18-21).
5. His ministry would include physical relief (Isaiah 61:1,2; see Luke 4:16-21).
6. He would be the Shepherd struck with the sword, resulting in the sheep being scattered (Zechariah 13:7; see Matthew 26:31,56; Mark 14:27,49,50).
7. He would be betrayed by a friend for 30 pieces of silver (Zechariah 11:12,13; see Matthew 27:9,10).
8. He would be given vinegar and gall to drink (Psalm 69:21; see Matthew 27:34).
9. He would be presented with all dominion over all peoples, nations, and men of every language (Daniel 7:13,14; see Revelation 11:15).
10. He would be hated without a cause (Psalm 69:4; Isaiah 49:7; see John 15:25).
11. He would be rejected by the rulers (Psalm 118:22; see Matthew 21:42; John 7:48).

The point should be obvious. Who is the only person who has fulfilled all of these prophecies and more? Only Jesus Christ. There is simply no way to avoid this fact.

Scholars Delitzsch and Gloag have rightly concluded,

So far as we can determine, these prophecies refer to the Messiah only, and cannot be predicated of another. The ancient Jews admit the Messianic character of most of them; although the modern Jews, in

46

consequence of their controversy with the Christians, have attempted to explain them away by applications which must appear to every candid reader to be un-natural ... these and other predictions have received their accomplishment in Jesus of Nazareth.... The combination of prophecies is sufficient to prove that Jesus is the Messiah....[85]

A Personal Word

The evidence in the Hebrew Scriptures proves that Jesus is the Messiah. God gave this evidence hundreds of years in advance so we would be certain to identify His Messiah. The Scriptures teach that the Messiah gave His life by paying the penalty of divine justice that was due our sin. Jesus the Messiah said, "For God so loved the world that He gave His only begotten Son, that whoever believes in Him should not perish, but have eternal life" (John 3:16, NASB). To receive Jesus as your Messiah, your Lord and Savior right now, you may pray a prayer like the following:

Dear God, I ask Jesus, Your Messiah, to enter my life and be my Lord and Savior. I recognize that You have dealt with my sins when Jesus died on the cross. I acknowledge my sin and ask You to forgive me. From this moment forward, I believe Jesus is the Messiah, and that He died on the cross for me. I believe He rose from the dead and is living now, and I place all my faith and trust in Him to be my Savior and Lord and to give me His eternal life. Help me now to trust You, live for You, and grow in my relationship to You. Amen.

Receiving Christ is a serious commitment. Please contact a local church where Jesus Christ is honored or the Ankerberg Ministry in care of this publisher for helpful information on living the Christian life. (Jews for Jesus in San Francisco also has important and helpful materials regarding the life of Jesus the Messiah.)

Notes

1. Malcolm Muggeridge, *Jesus the Man Who Lives* (New York: Harper and Row, 1978), 7.
2. e.g., Pinchas Lapide and Ulrich Luz, *Jesus in Two Perspectives: A Jewish/Christian Dialogue* (Minneapolis: Augsburg, 1985); Hugh J. Schonfeld, *The Passover Plot* (New York: Bantam, 1969); Gerald Sigal, *The Jew and the Christian Missionary: A Jewish Response to Missionary Christianity* (New York: KTAV Press, 1981).
3. Franz Delitzsch and Paton Gloag, *The Messiahship of Christ* (Minneapolis, MN: Klock and Klock, 1983), Book 2, 50-53.
4. Peter W. Stoner, *Science Speaks: Scientific Proof of the Accuracy of Prophecy in the Bible* (Chicago: Moody Press, 1969), 4.
5. Ibid., 107.
6. Ibid., 109.
7. Emile Borel, *Probabilities and Life* (New York: Dover, 1962), Chapters 1-3.
8. H.C. Leupold, *Exposition of Genesis* (Grand Rapids, MI: Baker, 1978), 164; cf. William Wilson, *Wilson's Old Testament Word Studies* (McLean, VA: McDonald Publishing, n.d.), 145; Walter C. Kaiser, Jr., *The Old Testament in Contemporary Preaching* (Grand Rapids, MI: Baker, 1973), 39.
9. Leupold, *Exposition*, 166.
10. Wilson, *Word Studies*, 57.
11. Delitzsch and Gloag, *The Messiahship*, Book 1, 26.
12. Kaiser, Jr., *The Old Testament*, 42; Leupold, *Exposition*, 170. See note 14.
13. Charles Lee Feinberg, *Is the Virgin Birth in the Old Testament?* (Whittier, CA: Emeth Publications, 1967), 22.
14. The *Targumim* (pl.) are ancient Aramaic paraphrases of the Hebrew Bible. The best known are the *Targum Onkelos* (3rd century A.D., on the *Torah*, the first five books of Moses), the *Targum Jonathan* (4th century A.D., on the Prophets), the *Targum Pseudo-Jonathan* (A.D. 650, on the *Torah*) and the *Jerusalem Targum* (A.D. 700, on the *Torah*). Although the Targums are dated A.D., Ellison makes an important observation in his *The Centrality of the Messianic Idea for the Old Testament*: "Early rabbinic Messianic interpretation merits re-examination. Very much of their interpretation of Messianic prophecy is, allowing for the difference created by the rejection or acceptance of Jesus as Messiah, the same as that of the New Testament and early Church.... Because the influence of Hebrew Christian propaganda, which must have been felt for at least two centuries after the resurrection, has been underestimated by most modern scholars, we have failed to realize how impossible it will have been for the rabbis to adopt Christian interpretations of prophecy, *unless indeed they had been there all the time*.... By the middle of the third century Hebrew Christianity had lost its dynamic power and was rapidly becoming a sect despised by Jew and Gentile Christian alike. It was therefore possible to allow traditional interpretations of prophetic scripture once again to be taught. (H.L. Ellison, *The Centrality of the Messianic Idea for the Old Testament* [Tyndale, 1953], 15).
15. Kaiser, Jr., *The Old Testament*, 42.
16. Alfred Edersheim, *The Life and Times of Jesus the Messiah*, one volume edition (Grand Rapids, MI: Eerdmans, 1972), 711; Feinberg, *Virgin Birth*, 22-23.
17. Leupold, *Exposition*, 170.
18. Willis Judson Beecher, *The Prophets and the Promise* (Grand Rapids, MI: Baker, 1970), 412-413.
19. *E.g.*, Arthur W. Kac, *The Messiahship of Jesus: What Jews and Christians Say* (Chicago: Moody Press, 1980), 40-48.
20. W. Gunther Plaut, et al., *The Torah—A Modern Commentary* (New York: Union of American Hebrew Congregations, 1981), 1466.
21. Delitzsch and Gloag, *The Messiahship*, Book 2, 135-136.
22. Plaut, et al., *The Torah*, 1472, 1766.
23. Delitzsch and Gloag, *The Messiahship*, Book 2, 114.
24. Kenneth Barker, general editor, *The NIV Study Bible* (Grand Rapids, MI: Zondervan, 1985), 7th Printing, 805.
25. Charles Briggs, *Messianic Prophecy* (New York: Scribners, 1889), 323.
26. David Baron, *Rays of Messiah's Glory: Christ in the Old Testament* (Grand Rapids, MI: Zondervan, n.d.), 263.
27. Francis Brown, S.R. Driver, Charles Briggs, *A Hebrew and English Lexicon of the Old Testament* (London: Oxford University Press, 1968), 631.
28. Wilson, *Word Studies*, 385, 386.
29. Josh McDowell, *Evidence That Demands a Verdict: Historical Evidences for the Christian Faith* (San Bernardino, CA: Here's Life Publishers, rev. 1979), 199; Pierre Barbet, *A Doctor at Calvary: The Passion of Our Lord Jesus Christ as Described by a Surgeon* (Garden City, NY: Doubleday/Image, 1963), 129-147; cf. C. Truman Davis, M.D., "The Crucifixion of Jesus," *New Wine Magazine* (August 1971).
30. In Moishe Rosen, *Y'shua: The Jewish Way to Say Jesus* (Chicago: Moody Press, 1982), 74.
31. Edersheim, *The Life and Times*, 718.
32. Brown, Driver, Briggs, *A Hebrew and English Lexicon*.
33. Briggs, *Messianic Prophecy*, 326-327.
34. Jacob Jartenhaus, *Famous Hebrew Christians* (Grand Rapids, MI: Baker, 1979), 38-39.

48

35. Baron, *Rays*, 265.
36. Merrill Unger, *Unger's Commentary on the Old Testament* (Chicago: Moody Press, 1981), 1167-1168.
37. Edward J. Young, *The Book of Isaiah, Vol. 1* (Grand Rapids, MI: Eerdmans, 1972), 323-324.
38. Ibid., 336.
39. Ibid., 330.
40. J.F. Stenning, ed., *The Targum of Isaiah* (London: Oxford Press, 1949), 32.
41. Delitzsch and Gloag, *The Messiahship*, Book 2, 115, emphasis added; cf. Edersheim, *The Life and Times*, 723.
42. Walter C. Kaiser, Jr., *Toward an Old Testament Theology* (Grand Rapids, MI: Zondervan, 1978), 217.
43. Transcript of television program, *Do the Messianic Prophecies of the Old Testament Point to Jesus or Someone Else?* Dr. Walter Kaiser, Jr. and Pinchas Lapide (Chattanooga, TN: The Ankerberg Theological Research Institute, 1985), 22.
44. Delitzsch and Gloag, *The Messiahship*, Book 2, 286-287.
45. Ben Blisheim, "Messianic Judaism—An Alternative" (privately published), 6.
46. Raphael Patai, *The Messiah Texts* (New York: Avin, 1979), 166.
47. Ibid., 167.
48. Baron, *Rays*, 225-229.
49. In Delitzsch and Gloag, *The Messiahship*, Book 2, 295, emphasis added.
50. Transcript, *Do the Messianic Prophecies*, 21.
51. Pinchas Lapide, *The Resurrection of Jesus: A Jewish Perspective* (Minneapolis: Augsburg, 1983), 7, 126-131, 137-150.
52. Baron, *Rays*, 78; cf. 90, 107, 116; cf. Theodore Laetsch, *Bible Commentary: Jeremiah* (St. Louis: Concordia, 1965), 190.
53. Laetsch, *Jeremiah*, 191-192.
54. In Barker, *NIV Study Bible*, 1160.
55. Baron, *Rays*, 78.
56. Ibid., 19.
57. Ibid., 78.
58. Ibid.
59. E.W. Hengstenberg, *Christology of the Old Testament* (MacDill Air Force Base, FL: McDonald Publishing, n.d.), 833.
60. Robert Dick Wilson, *Studies in the Book of Daniel*, Vol. 2 (Grand Rapids, MI: Baker, 1979), 138.
61. E.J. Young, *The Prophecy of Daniel: A Commentary* (Grand Rapids, MI: Eerdmans, 1978), 193.
62. Wilson, *Book of Daniel*, 106.
63. H.C. Leupold, *Exposition of Daniel* (Grand Rapids, MI: Baker, 1981), 427.
64. Harold W. Hoehner, *Chronological Aspects of the Life of Christ* (Grand Rapids, MI: Zondervan, 1977), 118.
65. For a more detailed analysis, see our book, *The Case for Jesus the Messiah* (Eugene, OR: Harvest House, 1989), Appendix Two and Sir Robert Anderson, *The Coming Prince: The Marvelous Prophecy of Daniel's 70 Weeks Concerning the Antichrist* (Grand Rapids, MI: Kregel, 1977).
66. Cf. Delitzsch and Gloag, *The Messiahship*, Book 2, 223.
67. In Ibid., 226.
68. Ibid.
69. Ibid.
70. Thomas Edward McComiskey in Frank Gaebelein, ed., *The Expositor's Bible Commentary, Vol. 7: Daniel—The Minor Prophets* (Grand Rapids, MI: Zondervan, 1985), 427.
71. Ibid.
72. Ibid.
73. Ibid.
74. Homer Hailey, *A Commentary on the Minor Prophets* (Grand Rapids, MI: Baker, 1976), 209.
75. Hengstenberg, *Christology*, 358-359.
76. Delitzsch and Gloag, *The Messiahship*, Book 2, 118-119.
77. Edersheim, *The Life and Times*, 735.
78. C.F. Keil and F. Delitzsch, *Commentary on the Old Testament in Ten Volumes, Vol. 10: Minor Prophets*, James Martin, trans. (Grand Rapids, MI: Eerdmans, 1978), 481.
79. Baron, *Rays*, 77.
80. Delitzsch and Gloag, *The Messiahship*, Book 2, 121.
81. Keil and Delitzsch, *The Minor Prophets*, 388.
82. T.V. Moore, *Zechariah, Haggai and Malachi* (Carlisle, PA: Banner of Truth Trust, 1974), 199.
83. Edersheim, *The Life and Times*, 737.
84. Moore, *Zechariah*, 199-200.
85. Delitzsch and Gloag, *The Messiahship*, Book 2, 123-124.